Fearlessly Devoted!

A Devotional
for
Soldiers of the King of Kings

Gateway Center for World Mission
A Million Missionary Movement
Envision, Equip, Mentor, Resource, Release

Kenneth Shirkey

Printed in the United States of America

ISBN: 979-8-9873593-7-2

All Scripture quotes are from the King James Bible except those verses compared and then the source is identified.

Address All Inquiries To:
THE OLD PATHS PUBLICATIONS, INC.
142 Gold Flume Way
Cleveland, Georgia, U.S.A.

Web: www.theoldpathspublications.com
E-mail: TOP@theoldpathspublications.com

The picture on the front cover is titled “The Last Battle” from Adobe Stock photos.

ACKNOWLEDGEMENT

First of all, I want to give thanks to the Lord and acknowledge that it is only by the Holy Spirit that the vision came about.

I would like to acknowledge my wife, Martha, for her enduring patience, contribution and editing that made this project possible. Additionally, to Bishop Josep Rosello, Tim Davies, and Kerry Dorell for their inspiration and input that encouraged me to launch this project. I also want to thank Pastor Carroll Parrish for encouraging me to bring the devotional to print.

I thank the Gateway Prayer Team for the covering and feedback as the draft version was circulated through the network. The war has been intense, and their covering has sustained my wife and me in ministry and the development phase of this project.

DEDICATION

I would like to dedicate this devotional to the many fathers in the faith that have labored for years to raise up warriors that would carry the Gospel to the nations. I would also like to honor to the fearless pastors and leaders in the nations that have opened their doors and hearts for me to both share and to learn from their example. Often their cost of the standing firm in the face of adversity is more than I could imagine. The fruit of their lives and the example of these fearless warriors is manifested in the pages to come. May the fire of the Lord that burned in them burn in you as you set the foundation for your journey.

Ken Shirkey, Director,
The Gateway Center for World Mission

TABLE OF CONTENTS

FOREWORD

Like it or not, you are involved in a war. This war is more than you can imagine. It is a spiritual war between the Lord and Satan and his forces of evil for the souls of men. Everything that happens in the spiritual world determines what happens in the natural world.

The Lord has won the victory but, by His design, He has left His church to enforce the victory and totally dispossess Satan and his minions. The Lord used the Greek term **ekklēsía** when he talked about building his church. The term is not a religious term; it describes a called-out group that was to govern. The Roman context was a group of people sent into a conquered territory to infuse the Roman language, its laws and cultural values into the people until the culture essentially became a Roman culture. The Lord didn't use the word Synagogue the Jews would be familiar with. The **ekklēsía** was given authority to establish the Kingdom of God on the earth and dispossess the principalities, powers, and rulers of the Kingdom of Darkness. Satan lost at the cross, but he doesn't give up ground easily. The war is not against people, it is against spiritual forces and requires spiritual weapons.

The battle is fierce, and it will require warriors who are fiercely devoted and trained for battle. To be prepared you have to know who God is, who man is, who Satan is and you need to know how to fight with the right weapons. The purpose of this devotional is to help establish you in your walk as a soldier of the King of Kings and to sharpen your sword so you can fight with understanding.

There are only two classes of people in the world; those who know Jesus and are part of his family and those who don't know Jesus and are not part of his family. If you know Jesus and are part of his family, you are hated by Satan and are seen as an enemy combatant that threatens his kingdom. He is at war with you. Therefore, if you are a believer, you are in the fight and called to be a soldier.

Soldiers are also in one of two groups: those who are engaged in the battle, and those living as if they were at peace and thus being overrun. Jesus commanded all his family to occupy or do his business till he comes back. He also said, "Be prepared, and *keep* your lamps lit." Matt. 25:7-13

Those who don't know Jesus and are not part of his family are already captured by Satan and are prisoners of war. They are destined to an eternity of suffering with Satan and separated from God forever. The good news is that Jesus loves them so much that he came to earth, took on human flesh, in fulfilment of the scriptures. He lived the life they couldn't live. He then died on a cross and rose again in fulfilment of the scriptures to open the way to be reunited with him forever. Salvation is a gift that can't be earned, only accepted. If you are without him, you can be free of any bondage and join his family by praying with a sincere heart:

Lord, I acknowledge that I am separated from you by my sin and that you died on the cross to pay the penalty and rose from the dead that I might be united with you forever. I ask your forgiveness for my sin and ask you to make me your child by coming into my life and changing me as only you can. I thank you for loving me and making me part of your family.

May the Holy Spirit bless you by giving you a spirit of wisdom and discernment to understand the battle you are in. May He bring you joy and victory in the battle.

Ken Shirkey, Director,
The Gateway Center for World Mission

FOUNDATIONAL VIEW

As we look around at the circumstances of the day, things seem pretty crazy. It would be easy to allow fear and anxiety creep into our lives to destroy our peace, our joy and our health. The world may seem to be crumbling around us, but we have to constantly remind ourselves of several things:

- **Our God is God and nothing else is:** not my understanding of him; not another religion; not the powers that seem to be at the helm. Deut. 4:35
- **He, Jesus, is the one who saves and nothing else can**: not the government; not my financial stability; not my own strength or abilities. Acts 4:12
- **He is the Creator of Heaven and Earth:** not some accident over long periods of time. Gen 1:1; Col. 1;16
- **He is the Truth, The Way, The Life:** not whatever seems to be right in my own eyes or any other individual. He is not like a man that He should lie. Jn 14:6
- **He is absolutely good: He is the same,** yesterday, today and forever**. Heb 13:8**
- **He has said that he has called you by name and redeemed you:** You are his. When you go through struggles, he will keep you. Isa. 43:1-3 He chose you, you didn't choose him. Jn 15:16
- **He has given me choices each day for life:** Elijah said, *"if the LORD be God, follow him"* 1 Kings 18:21

Joshua said to choose *"life or death."* Deut. 30:19 Every day, we have to choose:

1. To live, to serve God and trust in His faithfulness to keep us, to give us wisdom, and to help us walk according to His promise and character
2. or to follow things with our own eyes, our own understanding, my own emotions, and our own circumstances.

We should have the mind of the Psalmist when he says,

> **4** *Shew me thy ways, O LORD; teach me thy paths.* **5** *Lead me in thy truth, and teach me: for thou art the God of my salvation; on thee do I wait all the day."* ***Psalm 25:4-5***

DAY 1
WHO IS GOD?

Read: Ex. 33:18,19; 34:5-7

How do we know who God is? The world tells who they think he is, but who does God say he is?

The world sees a name as a differentiator like George or Sally. The names of God, however, all describe his character and what he does: El Shaddai (the all-sufficient one), Jehovah Rapa (the God who heals), Jehovah Shalom, (God our peace), Jehovah Sabaoth (the God of armies), etc. His name means who He is and reflects his reputation.

Moses' request was, *Show me your Glory* (kabod-weightiness). God responded by describing who he is by proclaiming his names. When we see His Glory, we see all that He is. 1 John 3:2

Reflect:

- Who do you say God is?
- How do you get to know Him?
- Knowing it is the Lord who works his nature in you, what steps can you take to allow him to come close?

Pray:

> ***23*** *Search me, O God, and know my heart: try me, and know my thoughts:* ***24*** *And see if there be any wicked way in me, and lead me in the way everlasting.*

Show me your Glory. Show me the difference between who you are and who I perceive you to be in my own mind. ***Psalm 139:23, 24***

Further Reading:

Lord, I Want To Know You, Kay Arthur, Waterbrook Press; The Names of God, Ann Springer, Zondervan

DAY 2

WHO IS GOD?

Read: Ex. 33:18,19; Heb 13:8

The Lord describes his nature as he hides Moses in the cleft of the rock. Moses had experienced the Lord and had an understanding, yet he wanted to really see him as he was (his full representation). It is interesting that in the Old Testament, no one could see the Lord face to face and live, so the Lord had to hide him in the cleft of a rock and show His glory from behind.

Jesus is our "Rock." Paul talks about being "in Christ."

> ***Colossians 1:27*** *To whom God would make known what is the riches of the glory of this mystery among the Gentiles; which is Christ in you, the hope of glory:*

He also states that,

> ***Galatians 2:20*** *I am crucified with Christ: nevertheless I live; yet not I, but Christ liveth in me: and the life which I now live in the flesh I live by the faith of the Son of God, who loved me, and gave himself for me.*

God has placed us in the cleft of our rock, Jesus, so his full glory can be seen in the world.

Reflect:

- What has the Lord said to you about himself in the Word and through the Spirit? Do you believe him? If not, repent for unbelief or for not believing fully.
- If God hid you in the cleft of the rock, what attributes do you think he would show you? What would you like to see?
- Write down three things you want to start believing about who God is?

Pray:

Lord, as I meditate on your word in Galatians and Colossians, plant deep within me who you are in me. Help me to reflect you in my daily life. Lord, I thank you for your faithfulness and that by your Spirit you will work out your character in me for your name's sake.

DAY 3

A COVENANT KEEPING GOD

Read: Gen. 15 & Genesis 22

Abraham believed God could do what He had promised him, but everything in the natural made it seem impossible. He asked the Lord, "How can I know?"

So the Lord initiated the most sacred of covenants — a blood covenant. In the blood covenant, participants would cut a sacrifice in half and walk between the halves in a figure eight pattern. As they did this, they would swear an oath that was binding on them and their respective families for generations. The figure eight pattern is often interpreted to mean that the oath was unbreakable. The oath was, "The Lord do to me as has been done to this sacrifice if I break the covenant." Each participant pledged all that they had to the other and to come to each other's aid if attacked. Both parties had to be willing and able to fulfill their part of the oath. The covenant was sealed with a meal of bread and wine.

The Lord put Abraham into a deep sleep. It was the Lord himself who passed through the sacrifice.

> ***Genesis 15:17*** *And it came to pass, that, when the sun went down, and it was dark, behold a smoking furnace, and a burning lamp* ***(terms referring to***

> ***God)*** *that passed between those pieces.* (my addition, KS)

Read

1 Sam 18:1-4-Covenant; 2 Sam 9:7 Generational Blessing

Reflect:

- Who sealed the covenant?
- How does the Jonathan/David covenant reflect the covenant given to you by God? 1 Sam 18:3,4
- What are some of the some of the traits that have been passed along to you from your past generations?
- What will you pass on? What part of God's nature will help you?

Pray:

Thank you that you are a God of covenant. Thank you that you have provided all that I need to walk in fellowship with you. I receive it and choose to walk in what You have done today.

Further reading:

Grandparents in Genesis, Lesley Barker Ph.D., Amazon

DAY 4

COVENANT KEEPING GOD-IT IS FINISHED

Read: Genesis 22; John 3:16

Abraham knew he was acting out prophecy. The Lord had said that through Isaac his promise would come. Isaac must have had great faith. Some say Isaac was around 30 at this point and could have said, "Whoa!" Both knew that the Lord had made covenant and would keep it.

What was the cost? Cost is often determined by the priority given to the covenant and the price paid. Most of scripture is devoted to the God's covenant redemption. The price was his Son. On that very spot some 2000 years later the Lord would literally fulfill his covenant promise with the words, "It is finished." He used the Greek word *teleō*, an accounting term meaning paid in full. There was no one else who could do it.

Abraham said,

> *God will provide **himself** a lamb for a burnt offering.* ***Gen.22:8***

> *For when God made promise to Abraham, because he could swear by no greater, he sware by himself,* ***Hebrews 6:13***

God swore by Himself because there was no one greater. Heb:6;13

Reflect:

Read 1 John 1:9; Rom. 5:8

- What about God's nature would cause him to keep His covenant?
- How does this part of His nature apply to you?

Pray:

Lord, I praise and thank you that though you see me as I really am, you sealed an everlasting covenant for me in your blood and opened the way for me to reconciled with you. I accept your gift and declare that I am redeemed. Help me today to walk by your Spirit with your strength and favor.

Further Reading:

Our Covenant God: Learning to Trust Him by Kay Arthur, Waterbrook Press

DAY 5

WHO IS MAN?

Read: Gen 1:26,27

There is a principle in studying scripture that says in order to get the understanding of a word, one has to go back to the first time it is used for the sense of its meaning or interpretation. This is certainly true when we try to understand who the Lord created man to be. Simply put, the image and likeness are to reflect what God looks like and to model his character. The Glory of the Lord was to be reflected in man. Christ was called the second Adam. It was said of him that fullness of the Godhead dwelt in him bodily. Col. 2:9

What was the Lord looking for? He had already created the earth and the creatures, but God was looking for a creature with whom He could relate and dialog. He wanted a family. He created man to be loved and to love Him back.

Reflect:

> *For whom he did foreknow, he also did predestinate to be conformed to the image of his Son, that he might be the firstborn among many brethren.* **Romans 8:29**

- How do I reflect what God looks like?
- How am I modeling His character?

Pray:

Lord, show me where I fall short of modeling and reflecting your likeness. I know that I cannot change and do this on my own. I ask, Lord, that you work in me all that is needed that the world could see your likeness in me. Ps 139:23,24

DAY 6

WHO IS MAN-WHY MALE, FEMALE?

Read: Genesis 2; Habakkuk 2:14; Eph 5:21-23

One flesh–different roles

> *Therefore shall a man leave his father and his mother, and shall cleave unto his wife: and they shall be one flesh.* ***Genesis 2:24***

God established the family as the basis of culture and a model Christ and His church.

By himself, man wouldn't be able to be fruitful and multiply and fill the earth with creatures like him. The knowledge of the glory of the Lord was to **fill the earth** as the waters cover the sea. Habakkuk: 2:14 Woman was a different helpmate than those of the animals. She was created in the image of God, just like the man. As they became one flesh, like the animals, they created a family after their own kind. Through these families the glory of the Lord would fill the earth. Paul says in Ephesians that the husband and wife are to reflect Christ and his church. Eph 5:32 Both have authority to govern in the family and on earth, but their roles are different.

Reflect:

- How does the image of Christ and His love

for the church impact your thoughts on the family?

- How does that impact your thoughts on family as the foundation of culture?

Pray:

Lord, help me to be part of the Bride of Christ (church family) so that your Glory will be shown and cover the earth. Help me to feel your love relationship with me as part of your family.

Further Reading:

Marriage as Spiritual Warfare, a teaching. Ken and Martha Shirkey

DAY 7

WHO IS MAN-FAMILY PURPOSE

Read: Genesis 1:28; Eph 5:21-31

It is interesting to reflect on why God created male and female. All of the animals up to this point were male and female. They created after their own kind. Man, however, was different than the others. He was created in God's image and was to represent God, to rule in the earth and to care for it. God wanted family with whom He could love, relate, and choose to love him as well. He ordained that the family unit be the basis of all culture. The bride/bridegroom relationship would model Christ and His church.

Before I was married, I knew about God and had a good relationship with him. However, it wasn't until I entered into a Godly marriage that I began to understand what an intimate relationship with him was. The scripture command of husbands love your wives as Christ loved the church and gave himself up for her took on a whole new meaning. In being a grandfather, I experienced a father's love for his children. The pain of being separated or losing them gives me a glimpse of the Father's heart for those who are lost.

Reflect:

- Are intimate loving relationships easy or difficult for you? Why?

- Have relationships in your life pointed you toward or away from understanding God's plan for family?

Pray:

Show me Your ways, O Lord, that I might walk with You. Thank you for being a relational God. Bring healing to the human relationships in my life so that I can receive Your created intentions for them. I want to walk in the light of Your truth today.

DAY 8
SET IN A GARDEN

Read: Genesis 2:15; Ps 115:16; Acts 17:26

God created man, male and female, to **reflect his image and character**. Scripture describes their time with the Lord as walking in the cool of the day. Their spirits were so pure and unhindered that they connected with God spirit to spirit.

The garden was lush and well-watered. It was an ideal environment that had been restored from chaos. It was a place where a family could grow and prosper. One of the first commandments was to be fruitful and multiply and to fill the earth with the knowledge of the glory of the Lord. Hkk. 2:14

We live in a fallen world that is but a shadow of what it was intended to be.

Reflect:

Acts 17:26 says that the Lord determines the time we were to be born and the place where we live.

- What is the garden he has placed you in?
- How are you spending time with him?
- How are you reflecting him in your garden?

Pray:

Lord, draw me close to you and work in me what is needed so I may walk with you unhindered and reflect your image where you have placed me.

DAY 9

MAN IN THE GARDEN-MODEL OF GOD

Read: Genesis 1:27,28; Genesis 2

The definition of ambassador is: an official envoy especially, a diplomatic agent of the highest rank accredited to a foreign government or sovereign as the resident representative of his or her own government or sovereign, or appointed for a special and often temporary diplomatic assignment.

While the earth is the Lord's and everything in it, he gave the earth to man as his responsibility to rule and care for in the same way He would. He gave him the authority to govern as He would. Ps 115:16

> ***Genesis 1:27*** *So God created man in his own image, in the image of God created he him; male and female created he them.* ***28*** *And God blessed them, and God said unto them, Be fruitful, and multiply, and replenish the earth, and subdue it: and have dominion over the fish of the sea, and over the fowl of the air, and over every living thing that moveth upon the earth.*

Adam was the representation of God. He and Eve were given the authority to govern and care for the earth as if the Lord were there. The Glory of the Lord was visible everywhere they went and in everything they did. Man was so connected with God that when God thought, Adam thought and responded.

Reflect:

- Have you thought of yourself as the Lord's ambassador?
- What authority have you utilized in your garden?
- Ask the Lord how you can better fill your role as His ambassador.

Pray:

Lord Jesus, thank you for your sacrifice to make me part of your family. Thank you for sending the Holy Spirit to empower me as I walk out my journey in the world. Lord, draw close to me and make me an ambassador that will reflect you as you are.

DAY 10

MAN IN THE GARDEN-AUTHORITY

Read: Genesis 2; Ps 115:14

Adam and Eve before the fall had unbroken relationship with the Father. They were abiding in him and were reflecting him unfiltered to the creation. Scripture declares that the heavens belong to the Lord but the earth he has given to man. Why did God do that? The tone of this statement is one of "lease for management." Man was charged to both rule and steward everything on earth. The Lord never gives a responsibility without the authority to fulfill His mandate. Ps. 115:14

> ***Matthew 28:18*** *And Jesus came and spake unto them, saying, All power is given unto me in heaven and in earth.*
> ***19*** *Go ye therefore, and teach all nations, baptizing them in the name of the Father, and of the Son, and of the Holy Ghost:*

Jesus said he could only do what he saw the Father doing and say what he heard the Father saying. Jn 14:10 The Lord gave the Holy Spirit to the disciples and those who believed on him because of the their words and gave them his authority in order to carry out the work of the Kingdom. John 17:20 They would literally do the things he did. John 14:12

Reflect:

- What has the Lord given you responsibility for?
- How do you think God would manage what you have been given?
- What authority was given to carry out your responsibilities?

Pray:

Lord, I realize that without you I can do nothing, but I thank you for the promise that you would always be with me. Lord, please help me to understand the authority you have given me and give me the wisdom and discernment to use it as you would.

Further Reading:

I Give You Authority, Charles Craft, Chosen Books

DAY 11

MAN IN THE GARDEN-RESPONSIBILITY

Read: Ps 115:14; Matthew 16:19; Matthew 18:18; Luke 12:48

It is an amazing thing to think about the Lord giving us dominion and care of the earth realm. Man is created in the image and likeness of God.

Adam was charged with naming the animals. He was called to cultivate and care for the earth. Work was established as an act of worship and obedience.

As God spoke and things happened, so too, man spoke and things would happen. He carried the responsibility of the impact of his words. Scripture says there is life and death in the power of the tongue. As God's ambassador, man has responsibility to use his authority by speaking in ways that would bring Godly results.

Man was given government as the representative of God in the earth to do business for him.

Reflect:

- Where has God given me responsibility?
- How am I using my authority to establish His kingdom on the earth?
- As God's ambassador, how am I using my words to bring life or death?

Pray:

Psalm 25:4 *Shew me thy ways, O LORD; teach me thy paths.* ***5*** *Lead me in thy truth, and teach me: for thou art the God of my salvation; on thee do I wait all the day.*

DAY 12

FALL-WHERE ARE YOU ADAM?

Read: Genesis 1; Genesis 3

The Lord and man walked in the garden in unbroken fellowship. What the Lord did, Adam did. Their spirits were joined. Why did the Lord, who knows everything, ask, "Adam, where are you?" It was not that he didn't know where man was located, it was to get man to acknowledge his condition. How often does the Lord ask a question to get us to think about some condition we are in?

The loss of the intimacy of communication with God was the greatest tragedy of the fall. The only time Jesus couldn't call God, Father, was when he was hanging on the cross and took the full sin of the fall onto himself. Jesus cried, *My God, My God, why have you forsaken me?* His unbroken relationship with the Father was broken by the sin of man.

Another tragedy was that man, like all creation, was designed to replicate after his own kind. Man in his original state would multiply like his original condition, but now mankind could only replicate the fallen state. Only after the resurrection, those "born again" in Jesus could once again replicate creations that had the direct connection with Lord. They would be spiritual sons and daughters, not just physical ones.

Read:

John 1: 1-12

Reflect:

- What does it mean to be a direct child of God?
- Has the Lord been calling you to come closer? How will you respond?
- You replicate who you are, not necessarily what you say. What are you replicating in others?

Pray:

Lord, search me and let me know my heart as you see it. Work in me the image of your Son that I might replicate him in others. (Romans 8:29)

DAY 13

WHO IS SATAN?

Read: Ezek. 28:12-17; Isa. 14:12-14; John 10:10

In order to know the nature of the battle, it is important to know the enemy, Satan. Satan now had control over man. Contrast the change of Satan's condition before and after his fall with man's condition before and after the fall.

Satan's Original Condition

- Son of the morning, anointed Cherub, servant of the most High
- Created being, perfect in wisdom and in beauty
- Access to coals of the altar of God, anointed cherub that covered, oversaw angels to carry out will of God
- Blameless
- Covered with brilliant glory
- Created to lead worship

Satan's Fallen Condition

- Fallen Attitude-I will ascend to heaven
- Fallen Attitude-I will raise my throne above the stars of God
- Fallen Attitude-I will sit on the mount of assembly in the recesses of the North
- Fallen Attitude-I will ascend above the heights of the clouds
- Fallen Attitude-I will make myself like the

Most High

His focus is to steal, kill, and destroy. John 10:10

Reflect:

- Who was Adam connected with before and then after the fall?
- How did Adam reflect the character of Satan after the fall?
- What do my attitudes and actions show me about who I am focused on today?

Pray:

I thank you, Lord, that you work in me both to will and to do your good pleasure. Draw me deeper that I might focus on your will and not my desires that you would be glorified. Phil. 2:13

DAY 14

CHRIST-THE SECOND ADAM

Read: 1 Cor 15:44-49; Matt 28:18-20

Jesus came to redeem us from the curse. Paul refers him as the second Adam. He was a restoration of the original state of Adam. It was a reestablishment of the mandate to be fruitful and multiply and fill the earth with disciples who reflect the Glory of the Lord.

He is our Kinsman Redeemer who restored our connections with the Lord and inheritance in the earth. Things to think about:

Jesus only did what he saw the Father doing and said only what he heard the Father saying– like the first Adam

Jesus said that he who believes in him would do the things he did and would do even greater things John 14:12

Jesus was the exact representation of God's glory Heb. 1:3 Adam was created in the image and likeness of the Godhead

The Father predestined us to be conformed into the image of his son Rom. 8:29

Reflect:

- If Christ in me is the hope of glory, what do I reflect?
- What is hindering me from doing the things Christ did?
- What is the Father saying to me?

Pray:

Lord, open my ears that I might hear you clearly. Give me boldness to act on what you say. Pour out your Spirit and do signs and wonders through me that you would be glorified.

Further Reading:

The Book of Ruth

DAY 15

IN CHRIST-A NEW CREATION

Read: John 1:12,13; Col 1:17; Gal. 2:20

Adam was a direct creation of God. Like in creation, the seed was in him to replicate after his own kind. That trait didn't change after the fall. Since the children of Adam came after the fall, all the children carried the fallen nature. Jesus came as a direct creation of God carrying the DNA of the Father, not human DNA. John declares that those who believe on him also become a direct creation of God.

Your DNA is from a new family. The generational things handed down from your natural family no longer have a hold on you. Natural things, both good and bad, can be passed down, but you don't have to be bound by them. Christ is in you. You have access to the Father and everything that He has. You also have the ability to carry out what the Father has commanded for your life. The real you is being transformed into the image of Jesus by the Holy Spirit. Like the unfallen Adam, you have direct access to the Lord and can walk with him in the cool of the day.

Reflect:

- How does the life you live today reflect the Christ living in you?
- How can you change your life to more align yourself with your new DNA? List three ways.

- What are things the Lord has blessed you with as you grow in your journey?

Pray:

Thank you, Lord for making me part of your family. Send your Spirit to help me grow fully and so to allow you to live your life through me.

Further reading:

Grandparents in Genesis, Lesley Barker Ph.D., Amazon

DAY 16
COMING NEAR TO GOD

Read Heb 11:6

It is pretty easy to get discouraged when everything around you seems hopeless and out of control. We often get busy doing stuff or trying to be the right person in order to please God and make it into heaven for eternity. Unfortunately, the more we try to be good or excellent to earn the favor of God, the more frustrating it gets because, quite frankly, in the flesh, we never will be perfect. That is good; No, Great News!! While many people believe that He exists, many don't believe that He loves them and wants to reward them for just following after him. We don't trust that he will do what says he will do. It may be that we think that He will do it for others, but not me.

The only way to truly please him is to believe he is who he says he is, and he does what he says he will do. His heart is for us and he will reward us for diligently seeking him in everything. Think of it: the God of heaven, the creator of the universe, loves you and wants a relationship with you. He longs to have you quit running after things that keep you from him. If you believe that he exists and that he rewards those who diligently walk their lives after him by his plans, your reward will be more than you can think or imagine.

Reflect:

- Ask the Lord to increase your faith and draw you near to him.
- Ask him what is on his heart and to show you how you can flow with that.
- Ask him to strengthen your faith and give you discernment to keep you from running after things that don't build the Kingdom of God in you and others.

Pray:

Father, your Word says that the steps of a righteousness man are ordered by the Lord. I acknowledge that it is your righteous that covers me and not my own. I ask you to order my steps and give me wisdom and discernment to walk in the Kingdom with your passion and anointing.

DAY 17

THE LORD WHO HEARS

Read: Ex 3:7,8a

Have you often looked to Jeremiah 33:3, *Call unto me, and I will answer thee, and shew thee great and mighty things, which thou knowest not*, when you need to understand the will of the Lord? It is comforting to know that the Lord actually hears our cries and answers us. The Lord constantly talked about asking, seeking, knocking.

It's like the story about a man who falls over a cliff and catches hold of a small tree on the way down. As he is hanging there, he cries out to the Lord. The Lord replies, "Trust me and let go of the tree." The man thinks about that for a minute and then replies, "Is there anyone else up there?"

How often it is not the lack of God speaking, but the dullness of our hearing. Hearing is more than receiving sound; it is coupled with action, trust, and obedience.

Reflect:

- What have you asked for that you have been waiting for some time without an answer?
- Have you asked, "WHY"? or have you asked, "What are you working in me"?
- Has the enemy told you that God won't hear your petitions?
- Do you believe that God answers prayer,

but cannot believe He will do it for you?

Pray:

Lord, please give me ears that hear what the Spirit says to the church and give me boldness to act on what I hear. Work in me the faith to believe you when you answer.

DAY 18

EYES THAT SEE

Read: 2 Kings 6:15-17

The enemy often orchestrates situations in the world around us to make you think he is powerful. He brings doubt that the Lord is strong enough to handle it. We live in a time when false information comes from the media, our educational institutions and even governments of the world. Evil is presented as more powerful and real than God's truth. Those who stand for Christ and the Word of God are increasingly at odds with the world. Efforts to silence them get very loud and strong.

Think on this: two thirds of the angelic host stand with us and have absolute power over the forces of darkness. All too often we look at our giants with natural eyes instead of the eyes of the Spirit and fail to step into all the Lord has for us.

Reflect:

- What areas of your life have seemed too big for you to overcome?
- Are there areas where the enemy has used fear to make you feel small or kept you captive?
- What can you do to strengthen yourself in the Lord?

Pray:

Lord, open my eyes to see you as you are and not as I want you to be. Open my eyes to see the world around me as you see it and the reality of the spirit realm as it is. Open my eyes to see me as you see me.

DAY 19

ENTERING OUR INHERITANCE IN END TIMES

Read: 1 Cor 10:11; Luke 10:13

There is a lot of press concerning terrorism in the world, both home-grown and foreign. The Lord shared with the disciples about the things they saw converging in the world around them. He also said that these events or things must come, but not to be afraid.

In 1997 the Lord gave me a dream that is being fulfilled in our time. The dream was a picture of three generations entering into the land of their inheritance. In the dream the first two generations were Israel. The third was the church today. The first and second generation of Israel faced similar issues we face as we strive to secure our nations and personal inheritance. Each generation had to war to dispossess giants in order to claim their inheritance, and we are no different. A dear friend once told me, "Without a battle there is no victory."

Reflect:

- What is the destiny the Lord has for you?
- What are the "giants" that keep you from receiving it?
- What strategy is the Lord giving you about the battle to defeat them and to obtain your inheritance?

Pray:

Lord, open my eyes to see You and Your greatness instead of the bigness of the "giants" that stand in opposition to Your plan for me. Give me boldness to step into the battle and confidence of victory by Your strength and power.

DAY 20

1ST GENERATION

Read: Numbers 13:27-29,31; 14:8-9,38,39

Twelve spies were sent out, one from each tribe, and scouted the land for forty days. They went through the whole land and brought back a sample of grapes that took two men to carry. The land was as God said it would be.

Ten spies saw things with their natural eyes. They saw the land was good but there were giants who had captured the land of their inheritance. They saw themselves as grass-hoppers and feared. Num 13:27-29

Two spies looked with spiritual eyes and responded differently. They remembered the mighty works the Lord had done and recognized that the giants were no different than the armies of Egypt. Num 14:8-9

God was not pleased with the ten. He said, "How long will they not believe me?" He was wounded and angry at their unbelief. God would fulfill His promise to bring them into the land, but only the two original spies who looked to God's ability obtained their inheritance. The others died in the wilderness and the Lord waited for another generation to fulfill his promise. Num 14:38,39

Reflect:

- How do see yourself in the face of the giants around you?
- How do you see God?

- If you see yourself small, what can you do to bring yourself into the "God believing group"?

Pray:

Lord, help me to see you as you really are and for me to see me as you see me. Only you can work in me the fullness of the Spirit and the boldness to overcome the giants. I choose you and your way. I trust you to do beyond what I can see.

DAY 21

2ND GENERATION-PREPARATION

Read: Joshua 1; Joshua 3

The first generation wandered in the wilderness until all who had despised the Lord through unbelief died. The second generation were born in the wilderness and now had a second chance to enter into their promised inheritance. Their journey required several things:

Provisions for the crossing

> ***Joshua 1:11*** *Pass through the host, and command the people, saying, Prepare you victuals; for within three days ye shall pass over this Jordan, to go in to possess the land, which the LORD your God giveth you to possess it.*

Focus on the Ark of the Covenant

> ***Joshua 3:3-4*** *And they commanded the people, saying, When ye see the ark of the covenant of the LORD your God, and the priests the Levites bearing it, then ye shall remove from your place, and go after it.* **4** *Yet there shall be a space between you and it, about two thousand cubits by measure: come not near unto it, that ye may know the way by which ye must go: for ye have not passed this way heretofore.*

Obedience to Follow Through

The priests carrying the Ark had to step into the water before the water would part and remain there until all had crossed over. Joshua 3:17 We often have to take a step of obedience to follow the Lord fully and enter into all He has called us to.

Reflect:

- What is your promised land or inheritance?
- What gifts and provisions has the Lord given you for the journey?
- Where has the enemy distracted your focus from the presence and direction of the Lord?
- What steps have you been shown to take but have not been obedient? What changes will bring you into obedience?

Prayer:

I ask your forgiveness for allowing distractions to get in the way of fully following you. Draw me into your presence so that I can see your plans clearly and passionately follow you fully.

DAY 22

2ND GENERATION-AN ALTAR OF TESTAMENT

Read: Joshua 4

In the relationship of God and his people, altars are key. The first thing Noah did when he came out of the ark was to build an altar for sacrifice. Jacob built altars in many places following encounters with the Lord. The Lord required that his altars be of twelve stones (one for each tribe) that no man had laid a tool on. Man is not to fashion an altar except according to his specifications.

The first thing the people of Israel were to do when they entered the promised land was to have a leader from each tribe take a stone from the middle of the river and set up a memorial. Two reasons for this were:

A touch point for future generations to remind them of the miracles the Lord had done for them vs 23

That all the world would know that the hand of the Lord is mighty and so that the nations would fear him vs 24

Reflect:

- What events have occurred in your life where the Lord worked to strengthen you?
- How did or could you build an altar? What has the Lord worked in your life as a result?
- How have you shared your testimony of the Lord to strengthen others?

Pray:

Thank you, Lord, for working in my life. Help me to let your light shine so that the world might see your work in me and through me and glorify the Father.

DAY 23

2ND GENERATION-PREPARING TO OCCUPY

Read: Joshua 5

The Lord gave the people of Israel grace during their time in the wilderness. None of the males born in the wilderness were circumcised. Circumcision was a mark that identified them as part of the covenant body of Israel. It is often compared to baptism. The people could now enter the battle in full covenant with the Lord. All the Lord has, including his protection and authority, was available to them in the battle. *Then the Lord said to Joshua,*

> *And the LORD said unto Joshua, This day have I rolled away the reproach of Egypt from off you. Wherefore the name of the place is called Gilgal unto this day.* **Joshua 5:9**

For the first time since the people's delivery from Egypt, they were back in full covenant with the Lord and were able to celebrate Passover in the Promised Land. They ate from produce of the land that they hadn't grown. The Lord protected them and provided for them in the journey. Now He would guide through leaders and his word. Two things happened that signified a new era:

- The manna stopped
- The cloud/pillar of fire no longer led them

The people would now have to function

in a new level of authority and take out the giants that occupied their Promised Land utilizing the Lord's power and direction.

Reflect: Read Isa 43:1-3

- What has the Lord required of you as part of his family?
- What authority has he given you?
- How has the Lord equipped you to secure your promises?
- What responsibility do you have to secure those promises?

Pray:

Father, I thank you that you know me even better than I know myself. You have called me by name and stand with me in the heat of the challenges that keep me from fulfilling all you have called me to. I choose not to fear, but to call on Your faithfulness. I ask for boldness to use all you have given me to occupy.

DAY 24

WHO IS IN CHARGE?

Read: Joshua 5:13-15

The men were ready. Their reproach had been rolled away. They were revived with food they didn't plant and they had the promise that this land was theirs to conquer.

Joshua, an anointed general, walked out of camp and met a man in the road with a sword in his hand. Like a good sentry, he challenged the warrior and said, "Are you for us or them?" The reply startled him. "Neither, but as the Captain of the Host of the Lord, I have now come." He said to Joshua, "Take off your shoes for this is hallowed ground."

Joshua had heard that before on the mountain coming from the burning bush as he accompanied Moses. He knew it was the Lord himself, so he did as he was commanded. Then the Lord preceded to give Joshua the battle plan for Jericho.

Reflect:

- Who was in charge?
- What has the Lord given you to do for the Kingdom?
- Have you put together a strategy to carry it out?
- Have you asked the Lord for His strategy?

Pray:

Thank you, Lord, for paying the price on the cross so the reproach of sin and death could be rolled away from me. Thank you for your Word that you will strengthen me and train my hands for war. Now, Lord, I ask that you make your presence known to me and show me **your** strategy that I might carry out all that is needed to win the battles in my life and bring you glory.

DAY 25

TAKE OFF YOUR SHOES

Read: Ruth

What in the world did, "Take off your shoes mean?" The Lord led me to the Book of Ruth. Boaz was a kinsman redeemer for Ruth. He couldn't redeem her because there was one who was closer in lineage and that relationship prevented him from directly exercising his right. In his culture, the closest in line took off his sandal (shoe) to relinquish his right to redeem.

What the Lord was telling Joshua was that he had no authority to carry this out. He couldn't accomplish the battle of Jericho in his own strength, or with his own weapons, or strategy. He had to relinquish to the Lord his right to carry out the battle on his own.

Reflect:

- Who fought the battle of Jericho?
- How will you defeat the giants that you face?
- Read Zec 4:6,7 How does it apply to what you are facing?

Pray:

Lord, I thank you that you don't command me to step up and conquer giants and expect me to do it with my own strength, power and wisdom. Forgive me where I have run ahead of you and tried to fight spiritual battles with carnal weapons. Teach me your ways and give me your understanding that I might partner with you and the angel armies you command. Bring Glory to your name.

DAY 26

SING A NEW SONG

Read: Ps 96: 1-4; Eph 4:14-16.

Expanding the Kingdom of God: This is a time of reflection and planning for the days ahead. Lord is calling us to sing a greater song in the nations. We are being challenged to expand and do what we have been called to do in new ways that will bring glory to God and life to people.

Years ago I worked with a man from Vermont. He was an avid skier. One summer, while mowing his lawn, his feet slipped under the lawn mower and he lost all of the bones in his toes. Most of us never think about toes in our body. They are usually hidden and often unattractive. The toes however are the agent of balance. My friend lost the use of his toes and thus his balance. Though he had the skills to ski, he couldn't hold his balance to make it down the slope. Often, it is the little gifts that bring balance to the body.

Each one of us has a song that only we can sing and a gift that only we can bring. It is when we all sing together that the Body of Christ is revealed and the Kingdom of the Lord is fully manifested. No gift is unimportant.

Reflect:

- What song is your life singing to the world?
- When people look at your life as a believer, how do they perceive God? Ask God to help

you sing a "new" song today.

Pray:

Lord, I am grateful that you have created me with gifts and a purpose that make my life unique. Make me an instrument of your glory and connect me with others that will amplify the song of the redeemed to show the fullness of Jesus to the world. May my life sing Jesus.

DAY 27

A TIME FOR WAR

Read: Eph 6:10-12

Our struggle is not against people, political parties, or nations. It is God against the evil spiritual forces of Satan who want to control the world and its people. The enemy uses fear and deception to manipulate people into giving him access to steal, kill, and destroy. Fear is, itself, a spirit that paralyzes and causes people to do things they wouldn't normally do or submit to tyranny.

It is not whether we are in war, but how are we engaged in the battle. Everyone who comes to salvation is part of the Body of Christ. That means that you are automatically an enemy of Satan and his plans. The problem is that most in the western church live as if they were part of a peace time army. Jesus said,

> *Think not that I am come to send peace on earth: I came not to send peace, but a sword. Matthew 10:34*

The Lord also said that you will encounter opposition, but that he has overcome the world. The Lord specifically stated that the main thing to watch in our time is to not be deceived.

Reflect:

Where have you become "comfortable" in

your walk?

- Can you identify places in your life where the enemy of our souls has brought leanness or destruction?

What steps can you take to build your wartime capability?

Pray:

Lord, show me where I have become comfortable as a peacetime warrior. I ask your forgiveness for giving the enemy room to steal, kill, or destroy in my life. I declare that will stop today and that you will work in me both the will and the ability to accomplish your good purpose.

Further Reading:

Spiritual Warfare Handbook. Chuck Pierce and Robert Heidler, Chosen Books

DAY 28
WEAPONS

Read: 2 Cor 10:3-5; Eph 6:18

Worldly weapons are not effective in changing the long-term outcome of any war. The reality is the spirit realm actually controls the worldly realm.

Several years ago, we were flying into the Dominican Republic to do a pastors' conference for Haitian leaders. Our host (a Haitian leader) met us at the airport and began to excitedly share of a miracle of intercession he had just experienced.

A group of Dominican intercessors had been praying daily for him and the conference. One night the Lord overshadowed the group and told them to pray for this leader and his wife until the Holy Spirit told them to stop. At the same moment, this leader and his wife were heading into Port Au Prince, Haiti, to deal with a Canadian visa for one of his family members. Suddenly, a group of robbers stopped the car, threatened to kill them and stole the car. One of the men started to kill everyone when his leader stopped them for an unknown reason. He simply said, "Let them go, they have children."

Two days later the Lord called on the Dominican intercessors to pray at the same time the leader was again going into Port Au Prince in a borrowed truck. Their journey took them past the police station, and there in the courtyard was their car. The police had gone into the gang area and forcefully taken possession of the vehicle. Our friends paid 50 Haitian dollars for the impound storage and were able to take their vehicle home.

God used the obedient prayers of the intercessors to save the lives of our leader and his wife as well as to restore their vehicle.

Reflect:

- What did Satan intend to do?
- Who were the targets and what was the effect?
- How can you sharpen your weapons?

Pray:

Lord, draw me close and speak to me. Give me eyes to see, ears to hear and a boldness to war with you to bind the enemy and to push back the darkness. Release the angel armies to deliver the nations from the evil one

DAY 29
BOLD AMBASSADORS

Read: Acts 12:4-17; Eph 6:19-20

There he was, arrested and scheduled for execution. James the brother of John had been killed with a sword and he was next. The door was being guarded by four men and there was no way out. But Peter was not alone. There was a home group fervently praying for him without ceasing. Suddenly, an angel was dispatched to Peter's cell. He woke Peter up and told him to follow him out the door. Peter thought, "Huh? What? Am I dreaming? The door just opened, and I am following him out of the jail into the street. I must be dreaming." As suddenly as he had come, the angel left. But here Peter was in the street a block from the prison. It was real.

Peter's home group was bold and fervent in intercession and an angel was dispatched to bring deliverance. The church in Acts 4 prayed for boldness to preach the gospel and that the Lord would stretch out His hand and bring signs, wonders, and miracles.

Bold prayer and intercession are the heavy artillery. It is the violent who take the kingdom by force; not in the natural, but with weapons of the Spirit—Word, prayer, with signs and wonders. One of the biggest strategies of the enemy is to wear down the saints. He tries to tell them that prayer is a last resort, or prayer doesn't matter.

Be bold and courageous! Declare God's word and ask Him to release angel armies to fight with the church army and occupy until he comes.

Reflect:

- Where have you felt captured or grown weary in pursuing what the Lord has put on your heart?
- How is your prayer life? Do you have a group around you that is praying for you?
- What steps can you take to set aside more time with the Master and be bolder in your walk?

Pray:

Lord, I praise you that you are ever for me and that, as your ambassador, you will work in me both the will and the ability to accomplish your good purpose. I pray you would give me boldness both to live and to proclaim the Gospel.

DAY 30

FIGHTING WITH BATTLE SENSE

Read: Eph 1:7-23

There is a difference between living in peace time and living as a soldier in war. The preparation for military service takes several steps. The transformation begins with basic training where individual civilians undergo a total mindset transformation to become part of a team. They learn military terms and discipline. New recruits live under a common code of behavior and authority. Once this is accomplished, the new personnel go to advanced training on weapons and specialty skill sets. By this stage much of basics have become second nature. The person has knowledge of the weapons, discipline, and even possible enemy tactics.

The real transformation doesn't take hold, however, until one actually enters the conflict. A battle sense is developed that is outside the formal training. Adrenalin is high, and close bonds develop with fellow warriors. Higher levels of discernment and awareness become normal.

Spiritual warfare is natural warfare on a higher level and is fought with different weapons. Strength comes from knowing the Lord at deep levels and responding to his commands with quick obedience. We must have that battle sense to look with spiritual eyes to know both the enemy and the battle strategy to fight him. It is also important to develop a close bond and unity with the fellow soldiers and angel armies that join us in the battle.

Reflect:

- Have you ever been in situations where things looked ok, but you had the sense in your spirit that things were just not right?
- Have you faced a challenge beyond your normal patterns and you just knew what to do?
- Have you ever felt isolated from other Christians in your sphere of faith?

Pray:

Lord, I ask you to train my hands for war and give me strength with your Spirit to handle the weapons that fit the battle. I ask for discernment and revelation to know you and those among whom you have called me to labor. Thank you, Lord, that it is not by might, not by power, but by your Spirit we fight.

Further reading:

God's Unfolding Battle Plan, Chuck Pierce, Chosen Books

DAY 31

AS THE FATHER SENT ME

Read: John 20: 21,22; John 14:12

It is easy to read through the Gospels and marvel at the miracles and say, but Jesus was God. Jesus promised that we would do the things he did, only more. That is a hard thing to get your mind around, but it is true. It is also a command with responsibility. The Lord breathed on them and sealed them with the Holy Spirit. Ten days after his ascension, the Lord sent the Holy Spirit so they would have the power to carry out the work he called them to.

Think of it, Christ is in you with the same power that raised him from the dead. Eph 1 Like Paul, the life you live is Christ in you. Gal. 2:20 The Lord didn't ask you to do it alone. He made you part of a body with gifts that you don't have. Where we all use our gifts together, Christ is revealed. Eph. 4

The Lord said that we would do the things he did and greater things. John 14:12 We often think of the signs, wonders and miracles, but we forget that doing the things he did also includes spending all night in prayer in the Father's presence, seeing what he was doing and hearing what he was saying.

He also sent an army of angels to carry out the will and purposes of the Lord. Jesus is Jehovah Sabaoth, the God of armies.

Reflect:

- If Christ is in me, how does my life reflect him?
- Where does the authority to do what He did come from?
- What steps can I take to spend more time with the Father?

Pray:

Lord. draw me into your presence. Help me see what you are doing and hear what you are saying that I might fully carry out your purpose for me in the earth and bring glory to your name.

Further reading:

I Give You Authority, Charles Kraft, Chosen Books:

Angel Armies, Tim Sheets, Destiny Image Publishers.

DAY 32

NOT OF THIS WORLD

Read: John 15:18-25

One of the realities that is often hard to get your mind around is that when you are born again, you are in a new family and that this world you live in is not your home or identity. The Book of Revelation talks about the kings of the earth and those who live on the earth. The reference is not about those who just live there, but those who identify with the world.

Jesus says that you can expect hostility toward you if you follow Jesus. If you are like him, reflect him, and live as He lives right where you are, those of the world around you will hate you.

The world is increasingly hostile to the Gospel and Christianity. In the words of the Apostle Paul,

> *For we are unto God a sweet savour of Christ, in them that are saved, and in them that perish:* ***16*** *To the one we are the savour of death unto death; and to the other the savour of life unto life. And who is sufficient for these things?* ***2 Corinthians 2:15***

We can take courage that:

Jesus has overcome the world, and our home is with him.

He is always with us, and the angel army

that stands with us outnumbers the enemy 2 to 1.

Reflect:

- What are your real priorities? Are they focused on the just living in this world or are they focused on the Lord's Kingdom?
- Where has the enemy used fear, distraction or deception to keep you from doing what the Lord has asked or standing up for what He says is right?
- What steps can you take to establish yourself in the Lord and to lovingly reflect him to those who would be drawn to him?

Pray:

Lord, I ask you show me areas that need strengthening in my life to stand and reflect you to a dying world. Impart your love and nature to me to be the fragrance of life to those who would be saved.

DAY 33

HE KNOWS YOUR NAME

Read: Isa 43:1

Have you ever been in a situation where things are falling down around you? If so, think on these things:

- The creator of heaven and earth created you. Before the foundation of the world He knew your days and created you as you are. Ps 139
- Jesus has redeemed you. He chose you, you didn't choose him. Jn 15 He paid the price on the cross to redeem you! He said, "It is finished." Jn 19:30
- He called you specifically by name and bought you with a price. You are his and nothing can snatch you out of his hand. John 10:28,29
- He has encouraged you to FEAR NOT. His love is a perfect love, and perfect love casts out fear. 1 John 4:18

Reflects:

- Where has the enemy lied to you about how the Lord feels about you?
- What areas of your life has the enemy brought fear to paralyze you from moving forward in the Lord?

Pray:

Lord, I thank you that you loved me so much that you went to the cross and took the punishment that I deserved. I thank you that no matter what I face you are with me like you were with Shadrach, Meshach, and Abednego. I confess that many times I forget your love and commitment to be with me in the face of the enemy's challenge. Help me to focus on you and receive the love and strength that only you can give.

DAY 34

HE IS WITH YOU IN YOUR STRUGGLE

Read: Isa 43:2

Have you ever been in a situation where you knew the Lord was real, but it seemed like he lived on the other side of the earth? Maybe it was through a tragedy, a sickness, financial difficulty or just a spiritual attack. You cried out, but no answer seemed to come. Then came the lies from the enemy: God doesn't care; you are not good enough; God has rejected you; or even God is not real.

It is interesting that these desert places seem to be the places where the Lord does the deepest work. Jesus was in the desert 40 days before he began his earthly ministry. Paul spent a couple of years in the desert where the Lord himself prepared him for a global ministry. Isaiah says "**when**" not "**if**" you go through the waters or the fire comes. God uses these times to refine us and help us allow him to work through us instead of using our own strength or understanding.

> ***Hebrews 4:13-15*** *Neither is there any creature that is not manifest in his sight: but all things are naked and opened unto the eyes of him with whom we have to do.* ***14*** *Seeing then that we have a great high priest, that is passed into*

the heavens, Jesus the Son of God, let us hold fast our profession. **15** *For we have not an high priest which cannot be touched with the feeling of our infirmities; but was in all points tempted like as we are, yet without sin.*

Reflect:

- Think of the "desert" places you have been through in the past. How did the Lord strengthen in you in the process?
- What lies do the enemy still tell you?
- What have you learned that strengthens you for your present challenges?

Pray:

Lord, I thank you that even when it seems you are not working, you are working. Help me remember your faithfulness and love during my dry times that I might walk fully with you when things are good.

DAY 35

HE KNOWS WHERE YOU LIVE

Read: Acts 17:26

Paul states in this passage that God determines our appointed times and the place where we will live. Have you ever wondered why you were born in a particular place? And why now?

God does not think as man does. He knows the end from the beginning. He also doesn't create by trial and error to see if someone will work in his plan. Think of it, of all the times and places God could have chosen you to be born, he chose you, created you as you are and put you in place for a particular purpose for you at this time. You are an essential part of what he is doing at this point in time.

He knew all of the struggles, all the people you would meet and all the strength that would prepare you for his purpose. Where you live is not just a location. It is all the relationships, challenges, and culture that sharpens who you are.

Reflect:

- Why are you here at this location and at this time in history?
- What gifts has God created in you?
- What would be left undone if you weren't born, or if you don't carry out His purpose?

Pray:

Lord, I thank you that I am fearfully and wonderfully made for such a time as this. I ask that you fill me with a fresh outpouring of your Spirit and give me bold obedience to accomplish all you show me to do. I want to fulfill all that you have created me for. Accomplish that in me, Lord.

DAY 36

HE KNOWS WHAT YOU NEED

Read: Matt 6:32,33

Do not worry then...seek first His kingdom and His righteousness, and these things will be provided to you. Matt 6:31-33

"It is time to gather the troops!" The word of the Lord came strong and urgent. We had two mission trips planned, but this was to be an urgent response in addition to our plans. We only had eight weeks to prepare and we were not given an agenda or a teaching like previous conferences.

The fact was that we didn't have funds for any of it. We scraped together money from savings and coupled it with frequent flyer miles to buy the airline tickets. It was a desperate time in Haiti, and many of the pastors coming didn't have money to even feed their families. The Lord said to just tell them to come.

We were to be responsible for the $5,000 needed for the conference and food aid the leaders would take back to their families. We were committed to prayer and obedience to go, but the Lord had to provide.

Two weeks before the trip an unexpected large gift came in that not only covered the total cost of the trip but provided for two other missions trips as well. The Lord got the glory and strengthened our faith. We knew that if we would be obedient beyond what we could see, the Lord would provide the means. Much more happened, but that is a story for another time.

Reflect:

- What has the Lord given you to dream that is beyond your financial means?
- What has the Lord done in past seasons to show himself strong to you?
- If God is the God of more than enough, what would be enough to meet all your needs and leave the "more than enough" for you to fulfill what He has shown you?

Pray:

Lord, I thank you that you are the God of more than enough for everything you require. I ask you to show me what would be enough to meet my needs so that whatever you pour out above that would flow for the Kingdom.

DAY 37

FOR SUCH A TIME AS THIS

Read: Ps 139:15,16; Acts 17:26; Esth 4:14

We are living in a time like no other. The Lord is birthing an awakening that will eclipse those that have gone before. Even in the midst of the conflict in the headlines, we are going to see the Lord move in a dimension the Apostles have longed to see.

Before all of your days came to be, the Lord had already written them in his book. He created all each one uniquely from all others. That is all you are and all you are not. Ps 139:15,16

God is the one who determines the time and the borders of our habitation. Acts 17;26

God has a plan for redemption and restoration, and he has specific things he will do. Every person will be needed to accomplish his work. So think of it, of all the times he could have chosen you to be born, he chose you to be born when he is birthing the greatest move of the Spirit the world has ever seen. Of all the places he could have chosen for you to live he, chose to put you right where you are at.

In God's thinking you are extremely important. He needs your gifts working right where you are. Esther had to make a choice to step into her call at the peril of her life or be silent and possibly perish. We have the same choice in our day. Who knows whether God would use us to save a nation.

Reflect:

- Have you had opportunities to speak up for the Lord and Kingdom values, yet remained silent?
- What fear(s) kept you from doing so?
- What lies has the enemy told you concerning your character, abilities, worth, etc. that keep you from fulfilling all the Lord has called you to do?

Pray:

Lord, I ask that you give me revelation of the opportunities you have ordained for me. Give me the boldness of Esther to step beyond my comfort zone to fulfill my destiny and your purpose for those who will be affected by my choices. I renounce a spirit of fear and other voices that keep me from moving for war.

DAY 38

PREACH THE GOSPEL, MAKE DISCIPLES

Read: 1 Cor 15:3,4; Matt 28:18-20; 2 Tim 2:4; Mark 16:15-17

The Gospel simply defined—1 Cor 15:3,4

> ***3*** *For I delivered unto you first of all that*
> *which I also received, how that Christ died*
> *for our sins according to the scriptures;* ***4***
> *And that he was buried, and that he rose*
> *again the third day according to the*
> *scriptures:*

The Gospel is powerful—Rom 1:16

> ***16*** *For I am not ashamed of the gospel of Christ: for it is the power of God unto salvation to every one that believeth; to the Jew first, and also to the Greek.*

The authority and the goal—Matt 28:18-20

> ***18*** *And Jesus came and spake unto them,*
> *saying, All power is given unto me in*
> *heaven and in earth.* ***19*** *Go ye therefore,*
> *and teach all nations, baptizing them in the*
> *name of the Father, and of the Son, and of*
> *the Holy Ghost:* ***20*** *Teaching them to*
> *observe all things whatsoever I have*
> *commanded you: and, lo, I am with you*
> *alway, even unto the end of the world.*
> *Amen.*

The sense of the Greek actually says "as you are going" I command you to make disciples.

The methods—2 Tim 2:2

> ***2*** *And the things that thou hast heard of me among many witnesses, the same commit thou to faithful men, who shall be able to teach others also.*

The Gospel results—Mark 16:15-18

> ***15*** *And he said unto them, Go ye into all the world, and preach the gospel to every creature.* ***16*** *He that believeth and is baptized shall be saved; but he that believeth not shall be damned.* ***17*** *And these signs shall follow them that believe; In my name shall they cast out devils; they shall speak with new tongues;* ***18*** *They shall take up serpents; and if they drink any deadly thing, it shall not hurt them; they shall lay hands on the sick, and they shall recover.*

Reflect:

- You replicate who you ARE, both what is good and bad. As people see your life, what will be replicated? Will signs, wonders, miracles be replicated?
- Not all are evangelists, but all are called to evangelize. Where are your opportunities?
- List places or people where you have opportunities to share the Gospel. Start praying for them.

Pray:

Lord, I need your power to live as a witness that brings glory to your name. Help me to see when people are ready and give me the boldness to share your life giving word.

DAY 39
FINAL THOUGHTS

Scripture: Genesis 5; Ps 115:8; Rom. 8:29,30

We were challenged to develop disciple-making disciples in the leadership of Uganda. When we asked the Lord what He would have us impart to them, he spoke clearly. We were to teach them:

- The **Word** because it defines God's nature and strategy.
- The **work of the Holy Spirit** because it releases the power and work of God.
- **The discipline of Prayer** because it develops intimacy with God who is the source of all power and authority. Prayer also merges the power of God and the strategy of God to produce the works of God.

Additionally, because God created us to multiply after our own kind, we replicate who we ***ARE***, not just what we profess to be. God's purpose is to work the image of Son in us. He works through the Holy Spirit to work in us both the will and the ability to accomplish his good purpose. Rom 8:29

Scripture also says that we become like that which we worship. Ps 115:8 Worship is a key weapon against the enemy. It matters who and what we worship because it determines who we are and who we become. Elijah said,

And Elijah came unto all the people, and said, How long halt ye between two opinions? if the LORD be God, follow him: but if Baal, then follow him. And the people answered him not a word. 1 Kings 18:21

DAY 40

YOU REPLICATE WHO YOU ARE

Matt 28:19- Make Disciples of All Nations

We have had an opportunity to discover what Adam was like and explore Jesus as the last Adam. It is a law that you will replicate who you are, good, bad, ugly, beautiful, spiritually and naturally. Man was created to worship and commune with the Lord. The fall broke the spiritual link with the Father yet man still was created to become like that which they worship. Ps 115:8

Make disciples in this scripture is a command. It was his last command. The command of making disciples or people who look like, act like and have the character of Jesus begins to make sense when we consider that the Lord purpose is that the knowledge of the Glory of the Lord will fill the earth as the waters cover the sea.

Our decision now is, "What do I do with it?" Paul says.

> *And the things that thou hast heard of me among many witnesses, the same commit thou to faithful men, who shall be able to teach others also.* ***2 Timothy 2:2***

As you move forward, you may ask:

- What does the Lord ask of me? Matt 4:18; Matt 28:19
- What will it cost? Luke 14: 26,27,33-If He is

first all other things will fall into place.

- What do I do? John 8:31,32
- How will I know that I am truly a disciple making disciple? John15: 7,8

Remember it is God who works in us both the will and the ability to accomplish His good purpose. You have to be available, but it is the Holy Spirit that will work it in you. Don't measure yourself by others. When Peter was restored, he asked Jesus," What about John?" Jesus replied, "Don't worry about John, I am saying to you FOLLOW ME."

Next Steps

Devotions are great for quiet time, but sometimes you feel the need for community to study in a different way. We all need community to support our path ahead and to stay strong in the Lord. If you can't find a group for you, consider forming or joining a GCWM online Zoom group.

We have had great success in Zoom Bible Studies. Ken participated in an international Zoom Bible Study in Exmouth, England for about a year. We have had weekly family prayer Zoom calls every Monday night for over a year.

If you would like to be part of a Gateway Zoom group, contact us. We will decide together the logistics and the topic.

Email:
ken.shirkey@gmail.com
martha.shirkey@gmail.com

ABOUT THE AUTHOR

The Rev Ken Shirkey
Director, Gateway Center for World Missions

Ken is married to Martha and is the grandfather of sixteen wonderful grandchildren who know and love the Lord. Ken received a midlife call to mission in 1985. Two things burned in his heart: nations and leaders. This call was not to a specific nation or people, but to see every tongue, tribe, people, and nation alive with Christ. Leaders were the key to see viable church movements and the cry for trained leaders was always among the top five needs listed in every targeted people.

Ken entered full-time mission service in 1989 working with the U.S. Center for World Mission to mobilize churches for mission especially to unreached peoples. In 2002 Ken and Martha formed the Gateway Center for World Mission with the expressed purpose of training leaders in the nations. Since then the Lord has opened the door to impact leaders in fourteen nations.

Paul writes in 2 Tim. 2:2

> *And the things that thou hast heard of me among many witnesses, the same commit thou to faithful men, who shall be able to teach others also.* ***2 Timothy 2:2***

The Lord showed him a key principle in training leaders is the reality that "**You Replicate Who You Are."** There has been an abundance of teaching from the western church, but many have settled for being students of knowledge instead of living disciples.

The Lord challenged Ken to have a vision that was bigger than he could do. So, he prayed and asked God for a "God sized vision." The Lord replied, "I want you to spark a movement that will thrust one million missionaries into the harvest." That vision will take more than one man, one organization, one generation to accomplish in the natural. It will require an army of **fearlessly devoted** warriors partnering with the Holy Spirit and angel armies. They will have to know their God, know the fullness of who they are, the enemy they face and the reality of the war they are in.

For more information contact:
Ken and Martha Shirkey
www.gatewaycwm.org
Email: ken.shirkey@gmail.com
martha.shirkey@gmail.com
Phone:
859.537.3412
859.537.3423

www.ingramcontent.com/pod-product-compliance
Lightning Source LLC
LaVergne TN
LVHW010116170826
845678LV00012B/2428

* 9 7 9 8 9 8 7 3 5 9 3 7 2 *